TERRORISM IN THE 21ST CENTURY: CAUSES AND EFFECTS™

Investigating the ATTACKS ON THE WORLD TRADE CENTER

LENA KOYA AND CAROLYN GARD

Rosen YA™

New York

Published in 2018 by The Rosen Publishing Group, Inc.
29 East 21st Street, New York, NY 10010

First Edition

Library of Congress Cataloging-in-Publication Data

Names: Koya, Lena, author. | Gard, Carolyn, author.
Title: Investigating the attacks on the World Trade Center / Lena Koya and Carolyn Gard.
Description: New York, NY : Rosen Publishing Group, Inc., 2018. | Series: Terrorism in the 21st century: causes and effects | Includes bibliographical references and index. | Audience: Grades 7-12.
Identifiers: LCCN 2017002775 | ISBN 9781508174554 (library-bound)
Subjects: LCSH: September 11 Terrorist Attacks, 2001—Juvenile literature. | World Trade Center (New York, N.Y.)—Juvenile literature. | Terrorism—United States—Prevention—Juvenile literature. | Terrorism—Prevention—Juvenile literature.
Classification: LCC HV6432.7 .K694 2018 | DDC 974.7/1044—dc23
LC record available at https://lccn.loc.gov/2017002775

Manufactured in China

On the cover: Smoke and papers escape from the World Trade Center on September 11, 2001.

Contents

Introduction

Over fifteen years ago, the lives of Americans were changed forever. Before September 11, 2001, many Americans lived with a false sense of security that large-scale terrorism would never come to their country. Before September 11, there weren't as many security checks or armed police and military forces around important landmarks. Few people in the United States imagined that they would ever experience a plane hijacking. And then all of that changed.

That bright, Tuesday morning, many American lives were shattered when two airplanes struck the World Trade Center towers. The attacks would continue. Two more hijacked flights were used as weapons by terrorists; one was flown into the Pentagon, in Washington, DC, while the other did not hit its intended target and instead crashed in a field in Shanksville, Pennsylvania. Nearly three thousand people lost their lives and over six thousand were wounded. But the attacks had devastating long-term consequences as well. The September 11 attacks ushered in a new age of fear, suspicion, and surveillance. The United States created a new department to protect the nation against any potential terrorist threats and began a new—and much criticized—program of surveillance to prevent terrorist plots. Perhaps even more devastatingly, the United States entered into two long wars in Afghanistan and in Iraq. While these wars officially ended, the countries have not yet been stabilized and American intervention is still needed.

The consequences of September 11, 2001, continue to this day. Families and friends of those who were lost continue to grieve their loved

Rescue workers survey ground zero following the September 11 attacks on the World Trade Center.

ones. More deaths have also been attributed to the attacks in recent years as 9/11 survivors and rescue workers have succumbed to pulmonary diseases and cancer from inhaling the toxic chemicals released when the buildings collapsed. Children born in the years after September 11 have grown up in a country almost perpetually at war. Nearly seven thousand American service men and women have died fighting for their country in

Afghanistan and Iraq. And many, many Iraqis and Afghanis have been killed or lost loved ones.

The actions of nineteen men who hijacked four planes on September 11, 2001, continue to reverberate today. While it may seem like these attacks happened a lifetime ago to younger generations today, it is important to memorialize those who were lost and to learn about what really happened that day. Understanding the tragic events of September 11, as well as their deadly consequences, will help younger generations to better understand the world they live in today. And perhaps it will serve as a reminder that we must fight against hatred everywhere so as to not allow history to repeat itself.

CHAPTER ONE

History of the World Trade Center

Anyone who visits New York City is first impressed—and even awed—by its dense concentration of buildings and, especially, its skyscrapers. The city's buildings are indeed impressive and their size and grandeur are testament to New York's—and the United States's—economic power. Of the most famous buildings in New York, the World Trade Center topped the list for many years. Unfortunately, this would make it a target for those who wanted to strike at the pride and power of the United States.

In the 1960s, the World Trade Center was designed to show the world that the United States was an important international trader. The idea was to build something that would be noticed. Certainly no one could miss two giant towers that were 110 stories high and dwarfed the city's other skyscrapers. They would be the tallest structures in the world at that time.

When the towers opened, fifty thousand people worked in businesses that were related to world trade. These included commodities trading, bond trading, US treasury sales, offices of foreign governments, broadcasting companies, the US Secret Service, the federal Alcohol, Tobacco and Firearms (ATF) division, and many city and state offices.

The World Trade Center wasn't all business. The Windows on the World restaurant on the 107th floor gave diners a spectacular view of the

The World Trade Center towers dominated the New York skyline for many years.

city. Elevators whisked visitors up to the observation deck in less than a minute. From there a person could see for 55 miles (89 kilometers) on a clear day. The shopping concourse on the bottom floor was the largest indoor shopping mall in Manhattan.

The towers attracted more than businesses and visitors—they inspired daredevils, too. In 1972, a skydiver landed on the south tower. In 1974, Philippe Petit fired a crossbow carrying a wire from the north tower to the south tower. With the help of some steelworkers, he attached a cable

and walked back and forth between the towers for an hour. A judge later sentenced him to perform for children in city parks to atone for his crime. In 1977, George Willig used climbing equipment to scale the south tower. A judged fined him $1.10—one penny for each story he had climbed.

Many people didn't like the World Trade Center towers. They thought they were boring, that the towers stuck out and didn't enhance the surrounding area. In spite of the critics, the towers came to define New York City's skyline.

Americans looked at the World Trade Center towers and saw symbols of the openness of American society. A group of terrorists, however, saw the towers as symbols of the things they hated about America.

THE TOP OF THE WORLD

The World Trade Center complex was so large that it occupied a 16-acre (6.5-hectare) area in downtown Manhattan and had its own zip code: 10048. In addition to the World Trade Center towers (known as One and Two World Trade Center), there were five other buildings in the complex. Three World Trade Center was a twenty-two-floor hotel. Four and Five World Trade Center were low-rise office buildings, and Six World Trade Center housed the United States Customs Service and the US Commodities Exchange. Seven World Trade Center was a forty-seven-floor office building.

The Roots of Islamic Terrorism

These terrorists followed a very narrow interpretation of Islam. Islam is a monothesistic religion like Judaism and Christianity, which means that Muslims believe in one god. The original meaning of the word Islam is "submission" or "surrender" and refers to the religious belief that one should surrender to God's will. Nearly one quarter of the world's population follows Islam and nearly all of these Muslims do not commit illegal or violent acts based on their religious beliefs. Unfortunately, a very few, including Ramzi Yousef, a Sunni Muslim, go on to commit acts of terrorism.

Sunni Muslims believe that Muslims should try to live a life that mirrors the life of the Prophet Muhammad, the founder of Islam. About 90 percent of the Muslims in the world are Sunnis. The other 10 percent are Shiites, who disagreed with Sunnis early on in the history of Islam over who should follow in the Prophet Muhammad's footsteps as leader of the Islamic community. Ramzi Yousef's father belonged to an extreme group of Sunnis who thought that all Shiites should be killed. As Yousef grew up, these extreme views were impressed upon him. In 1986, Yousef moved to Great Britain and became friends with members of the Muslim Brotherhood, a group that supported terrorism.

Meanwhile, a war against the Soviet Union had started in Afghanistan. The Afghan government had changed, and the new leaders showed an interest in making an agreement with the United States. At that time, the Soviets were bitter enemies with the United States. The Soviets feared that under such an agreement the United States would establish a military base in Afghanistan. To protect their holdings, the Soviets sent troops to Afghanistan in 1979.

Many Muslims hated the Soviet Union because they considered the nation to be godless. Thousands of young Muslim men from around the world came to Afghanistan to join the mujahideen, or freedom fighters. Over the ten years of the war, more than twenty-five thousand mujahideen from thirty-five countries fought for Afghanistan. The United States, anxious to see the Soviets stopped, supported the mujahideen with $500 million and supplied them with guns, missiles, and training.

Ramzi Yousef joined the mujahideen in 1988. He spent several months in a training camp in Pakistan leaning how to make bombs. The camp was financed by a wealthy Muslim named Osama bin Laden. Bin Laden used his money to train the mujahideen to fight the Soviets.

The war proved disastrous for the Soviet Union. Even though it was the stronger nation, its troops weren't accustomed to fighting in a mountainous country against rebellious guerillas. In 1989, after

The mujahideen fought against the Soviets in Afghanistan during the Soviet-Afghan War from 1979 to 1989.

losing fourteen thousand men, the Soviet Union pulled its troops out of Afghanistan. Once the Soviet threat had vanished, the United States dropped all support of the Muslim rebels. This action turned many mujahideen against the United States. They returned to their homelands and spread their fundamentalist and militant ideas.

Yousef had many Palestinian friends, and he came to believe that the troubles of the Middle East were caused by Israel's oppression of the Palestinians. Since the United States is a major supporter of Israel, Yousef turned his hatred toward the United States. He was no longer fighting for his religious or political beliefs, but out of the desire to punish his enemies. He decided that his method of punishment would be to kill huge numbers of American people. He hoped to make these numbers as high as the deaths from the atomic bomb that the Americans had dropped on Hiroshima, Japan, in 1945, killing seventy-five thousand people. Yousef's plan was to make one of the World Trade Center towers fall onto the other. Both would crash to the ground, killing over two hundred thousand people.

The 1993 World Trade Center Bombing

To carry out his plot, Yousef moved to New York City in September 1992. Together with another man, Mohammed Salameh, he kept explosives in a rented storage locker. For several months the two men carried explosives to their apartment and worked on making a bomb out of urea (fertilizer), nitric acid, and sulfuric acid.

When the bomb was ready, the two men rented a yellow Ford Econoline van. They packed the bomb into this van. To avoid being traced to the crime, the terrorists reported the van missing ahead of time. Salameh called the police and told them that the van had been stolen from a shopping center parking lot. Just after noon on February 26, 1993, Yousef and a friend drove the van into the underground parking garage of the World Trade Center. Yousef lit the fuses and the two men left the smoldering van. At 12:17 the fuses burned down to the blasting caps.

The explosion moved at 5,000 miles per hour (8,047 kilometers/hour) through the garage. The shock wave from the blast bounced off the base of the north tower. The vertical steel frame didn't move, but the obstacle increased the force of the explosion. The wave roared through the parking garage, destroying everything in its path. The explosion went up several stories before it finally vented out of an entrance ramp in the garage.

Victims of the 1993 World Trade Center bombing are treated on the streets of lower Manhattan on February 26, 1993.

The bomb ripped a hole in the wall of a subway station, sending concrete and metal flying. Cinder blocks turned into dust. A steel fire door blew off its hinges and smashed into a wall 35 feet (11 meters) away. Three levels of steel-reinforced concrete floors were blasted away, leaving a hole 150 feet (46 m) in diameter in the basement. Following the explosion, 200,000 cubic feet (5,663 cubic meters) of water and sewage poured in, creating a lake 18 inches (46 centimeters) deep across the lowest level.

The first rescue units arrived within minutes. At about 11:25 p.m. occupants were taken out of the last elevator. They had been trapped inside the building for almost twelve hours. At 2:25 a.m. on Saturday, February 27, the incident was declared under control. Six people had died and over one thousand were injured.

The Investigation

The investigators found a piece of the rented van with the vehicle identification number on it. They traced the van back to the rental company. Salameh, who had rented the van, wanted to get his deposit back so he could buy an airplane ticket out of the country. When Salameh returned to get his money he talked with an FBI agent posing as a loss prevention employee for the rental car company. As Salameh left the rental office, FBI agents arrested him.

$2,000,000

REWARD

At approximately 12 noon on February 26, 1993, a massive explosion rocked the World Trade Center in New York City, causing millions of dollars in damage. The terrorists who bombed the World Trade Center murdered six innocent people, injured over 1,000 others, and left terrified school children trapped for hours in smoke filled elevators.

Following the bombing, law enforcement officials obtained evidence which led to the indictments and arrests of several suspected terrorists involved in the bombing. RAMZI AHMED YOUSEF, one of those indicted, fled the United States immediately after the bombing to avoid arrest. YOUSEF is now a fugitive from justice. YOUSEF was born in Iraq or Kuwait, possesses Iraqi and Pakistani passports, and also claims to be a citizen of the United Arab Emirates. Because of the nature of the crimes for which he is charged, YOUSEF should be considered armed and extremely dangerous.

The United States Department of State is offering a reward of up to $2,000,000 for information leading to the apprehension and prosecution of YOUSEF. If you have information about YOUSEF or the World Trade Center bombing, contact the authorities, or the nearest U.S. embassy or consulate. In the United States, call your local office of the Federal Bureau of Investigation or 1-800-HEROES1, or write to:

HEROES
Post Office Box 96781
Washington, D.C. 20090 – 6781
U.S.A.

RAMZI AHMED YOUSEF

DESCRIPTION

DATE OF BIRTH:	May 20, 1967 and/or April 27, 1968
PLACE OF BIRTH:	Iraq, Kuwait, or United Arab Emirates
HEIGHT:	6'
WEIGHT:	180 pounds
BUILD:	medium
HAIR:	brown
EYES:	brown
COMPLEXION:	olive
SEX:	male
RACE:	white
CHARACTERISTICS:	sometimes is clean shaven
ALIASES:	Ramzi A. Yousef, Ramzi Ahmad Yousef, Ramzi Yousef, Ramzi Yousef Ahmad, Ramzi Yousef Ahmed, Rasheed Yousef, Rashid Rashid, Rashed, Kamal Ibraham, Kamal Abraham, Abraham Kamal, Muhammad Azan, Khurram Khan, Abdul Basit

Ramzi Yousef was added to the FBI's Ten Most Wanted List before he was captured in February 1995.

After searching Salameh's apartment, the FBI found enough evidence to arrest other conspirators. Four of these men were sentenced to 240 years in prison, the number of years the judge thought the six people who died would have lived. Yousef and the man who drove the van had left the country the night of the bombing. For two years, FBI agents tracked Yousef around the world as he took part in other terrorist activities. In 1995, Yousef was arrested in Pakistan. Six months later the driver of the van was arrested in Jordan. Both men were brought back to the United States for trial. The juries found them guilty. Like the other conspirators, they were sentenced to 240 years in prison. Yousef is now in a maximum-security prison, where he lives in a small cell in solitary confinement.

As the plane bringing Yousef back to the United States flew over New York City, Bill Gavin, the head of the FBI in New York, showed him the World Trade Center towers. "Look down there," he said. "They're still standing."

Yousef replied, "They wouldn't be if I had had enough money and explosives."

CHAPTER TWO

The September 11 Terrorist Attacks

Tuesday, September 11, 2001, began like any other day. People headed to work in their cars, on subways, or on trains. Some people were scheduled for early morning flights. The sky was clear and there were no weather-related delays. In Boston, ninety-two people boarded American Airlines Flight 11 to Los Angeles. They were travelling for business, to take their families on vacation, and to visit friends and loved ones. The plane departed at 7:59 a.m., right on schedule. Fifteen minutes later, United Flight 175 also took off from Boston's Logan International Airport carrying sixty-five people onboard. The flights went as scheduled for the first fifteen minutes. Then, men carrying box cutters hijacked both planes and turned them toward New York City.

New Yorkers were enjoying a beautiful late-summer morning in the city. In lower Manhattan, many startled people looked up as the sound of a low-flying jet caught their attention. Planes weren't authorized to come so close to the towers. As horrified onlookers screamed, American Airlines Flight 11 flew directly into the north tower. The time was 8:45 a.m.

Black smoke poured out of the gaping hole in the side of the tower at about the ninety-fifth floor. Rescue workers raced to the scene. Inside the north tower, people headed for the stairs. Survivors reported that the evacuation went very smoothly. People helped one another down the long,

United Airlines Flight 175 flies into the south tower of the World Trade Center. It is the second flight, after American Airlines Flight 11, to fly into the towers.

dark flights of stairs. Many made it to the ground from the upper floors in just twenty minutes. Firefighters and police officers went in the opposite direction, up the stairs, to help with the evacuation. On the streets, crowds poured out of office buildings to stare at the tower on fire.

When workers in the south tower heard the crash, many of them started for the stairs. A public-address announcement assured them that the south tower was safe. Only the north tower had been damaged and there was no need to evacuate. Some workers went down the stairs anyway; others went back to their offices.

Coordinated Terror

Many people who knew Flight 11 had crashed into the World Trade Center, including government officials, thought it had to be an accident. The idea that this was a long-planned terrorist attack wasn't yet a possibility in their minds. This lasted for eighteen minutes. Then, all doubt that this was a serious terrorist attack disappeared: United Flight 175 flew directly into the south tower on live television. The plane hit the tower around the eighty-third floor and exploded into a giant orange fireball. Government officials scrambled to deal with what was now surely an organized terrorist attack—the worst ever on American soil.

The terror wasn't over. At 9:00 a.m. American Airlines Flight 77, with sixty-four people aboard, left Dulles Airport in Virginia, headed for Los Angeles. At 9:43 the plane crashed into the Pentagon. Twenty-four thousand people worked in the five-sided government building, including the secretary of defense. Flames and smoke rose from the western side of the building; part of it soon collapsed.

Fighter jets took to the skies, searching for more hijacked planes. The FAA ordered all planes in US air space to land immediately.

Fearful that other government buildings were targeted, the White House, the Supreme Court, the Treasury, the State Department, and the Capitol were evacuated. Across the country potential targets closed, including the United Nations, the Sears Tower in Chicago, the Space Needle in Seattle, Disney World, and the Kennedy Space Center. Most shopping malls, movie theaters, ballparks, and other places that attracted crowds closed.

In New York City, rescue workers ran into the south tower. They didn't have much time. At 9:50 a.m., less than an hour after it had

The south tower of the World Trade Center collapses.

been hit, the south tower collapsed onto itself. Thousands of employees and rescue workers never made it out of the building. People on the street heard the deafening whoosh. They ran north, away from the scene. Smoke and grit made it almost impossible to breathe or see. Those who made it out of the danger zone were covered in ashes from head to toe.

A plane crashed in rural Pennsylvania, 85 miles (137 km) from Camp David, the presidential retreat, at 10:10 a.m. While newscasters tried to make sense of this fourth crash, the north tower of the World Trade Center collapsed. The structure had handled the impact of an airplane hitting it, but the steel skeleton could not withstand the intense heat of a full tank of burning jet fuel. The columns melted and the building collapsed under its own weight.

The airplanes, filled with about 35,000 gallons (132,489 liters) of jet fuel for their cross-country flights, released 1.2 kilotons of energy, about one-tenth of the energy in the atomic bomb that was dropped on Hiroshima, Japan. The temperatures in the towers probably reached 4,000 degrees Fahrenheit (2,204 degrees Celsius). The steel simply wasn't able to handle the heat.

On the streets of Manhattan, sirens blared as people ran for their lives. Dust, ash, and falling debris filled the air. Office papers floated across the East River.

Less than two hours after the first plane hit the north tower, all that remained of the World Trade Center towers was a nine-story pile of rubble. In the middle of the afternoon, another, smaller World Trade Center building—Seven World Trade Center—collapsed. The Marriott Hotel at Three World Trade Center burned. At least ten other buildings sustained enough damage to make them unsafe.

The nation was stunned. Nothing of this magnitude had ever happened on United States soil.

SURVIVORS

Although emergency personnel and rescue workers had hoped, immediately after the attack, that there would be many survivors in the rubble of the collapsed World Trade Center towers, this was not the case. In fact, only eighteen survivors were found following the collapse.

(continued on the next page)

Genelle Guzman McMillan was the final person rescued from ground zero just after noon on September 11, 2001.

(continued from the previous page)

Twelve were firefighters who had been trapped in the north tower stairway, which fell around them while protecting them in a small air pocket. They were able to escape several hours after the towers fell. Genelle Guzman McMillan, who worked for the Port Authority, was the eighteenth and final person rescued from ground zero just after noon on September 12.

New York City's mayor, Rudolph Giuliani, closed all the bridges and tunnels coming into the city. Only emergency vehicles could enter lower Manhattan. Subway service stopped. City buses carried firefighters and police officers to the scene. Thousands walked across the bridges to Brooklyn to escape the smoke and dust.

Understanding the Attacks

Very quickly, intelligence agents and government officials knew that this was a coordinated terrorist attack. But they still needed to piece together who had committed these crimes and how they had done so. It became apparent very quickly that all four planes had been hijacked. Using phone calls from the hijacked flights as evidence, intelligence agents knew that the hijackers had taken control of the planes using only small knives. They also knew that the passengers on the plane in Pennsylvania, having learned of the earlier crashes, had staged a counterattack and had overpowered the hijackers. Although the plane did crash, it didn't hit its intended target, which may have been either the Capitol Building or the White House.

Aviation experts were also convinced that the planes that hit the World Trade Center were not being flown by their commercial pilots by the time they crashed. A commercial pilot would have been trained to fly the plane into the ocean instead of slamming it into a building. They also said that the hijackers had some knowledge of how to fly planes. Although the hijackers didn't need to know how to take off and land, they knew how to turn and how to keep flying at a certain altitude.

Night came, and with it a sort of calmness. Rescue workers continued to sift through the debris in New York City and Washington. Hope that anyone would be found alive faded as the hours wore on. Many workers found only parts of bodies. All the remains were put into body bags. In New York, refrigerated trucks took the bags to the medical examiner's office, where forensics experts set about the difficult task of identifying the remains.

Families of the victims took photographs and fliers from hospital to hospital trying to find their loved ones. They filled out long forms with details about the missing, such as dental records, scars, tattoos, and jewelry.

Two weeks after the attack, the number of the missing in New York was about five thousand, including those on the planes and the firefighters and police officers who had gone into the building. One-hundred-eighty-nine people at the Pentagon, both on the plane and in the building, had died.

In Washington, DC, FBI investigators examined the debris at the Pentagon. The rubble was then trucked to a parking lot, where crime scene technicians sorted through it. The process took a month. Since the Pentagon was considered to be a crime scene, officials did not make public everything they found.

For the first two weeks, the mission in New York City was classified as a rescue operation, and debris was moved carefully in case anyone could be found alive. When hope of finding any survivors was abandoned, the

New Yorkers walk past a wall featuring posters of those missing after the September 11 attacks.

operation changed to cleanup. Large cranes came in to lift the debris in huge scoops. Barges took the rubble to a 3,000-acre (1,214-ha) landfill on Staten Island. There, the FBI searched for evidence and parts of the airplanes. Eventually the debris would fill one hundred thousand dump trucks. Recovery and cleanup would continue until the site was cleared in May 2002 and cost a total of $600 million.

CHAPTER THREE

Immediate Responses

President Bush was reading a book to elementary school students in Florida when his chief of staff came into the room and whispered that there was a coordinated attack on the World Trade Center. To not cause unnecessary panic, President Bush finished reading the book and then gave a short speech about the attacks to the press. Shortly before 10 a.m., he was aboard Air Force One, the official presidential plane. Fighter jets escorted the plane as it flew to a

Andrew Card, President George W. Bush's chief of staff, delivers the news that the United States is under attack.

safe location in Louisiana. The president's location was top secret as he was a potential target for additional terrorists. President Bush returned to Washington at 7 p.m. that night, where he hid in a secured bunker under the White House.

Federal officials moved quickly to safeguard the nation. Donald Rumsfeld, the secretary of defense, was in the Pentagon when it was hit. He visited the scene of destruction before going to the National Military Command Center on the lower floors of the Pentagon. The Secret Service stationed armed agents on the roof of the White House.

Dale Watson, the FBI counterterrorist chief, activated the Strategic Information Operations Center (SIOC). Located on the fifth floor of the J. Edgar Hoover Building in Washington, the room has a secure communications system. FBI agents searched through intelligence reports to see if they had missed any clues that would have warned them of the attack. They looked for coded telephone messages, such as "There is a wedding tomorrow," or "You should come home." Nothing stood out. Over seven thousand FBI agents worked on the investigation.

Throughout the day federal officials held news conferences to keep the American public and the world informed. On the evening of September 11, the president spoke to the nation. In the speech he said, "I've directed the full resources for our intelligence and law enforcement communities to find those responsible and bring them to justice. We will make no distinction between the terrorists who committed these acts and those who harbor them." He ended the speech by saying, "None of us will ever forget this day, yet we go forward to defend freedom and all that is good and just in our world."

For the next two days the only planes allowed in the air were military jets patrolling the skies over major metropolitan areas. People found the quiet to be both refreshing and frightening. The airports were closed not only to prevent more hijackings, but also to prevent any terrorists from leaving the country (as two of them had done following the 1993 World Trade Center bombing).

Preventing Further Terrorism

Two days later the nation's airports reopened under very strict controls. The new rules included no curbside check-ins, random searches of vehicles entering parking garages, no vehicles parked within 75 feet (22 m) of the terminal, no plastic knives at food outlets in airports, extensive searches of luggage, no nail clippers in carry-on bags, and only ticketed passengers allowed on the concourses. The result, of course, was long lines. Most of the passengers gladly put up with the waits for the increase in security.

A week later, the FBI found a manual about crop dusting in a terrorist hideout. The investigators thought that the terrorists planned to use crop dusting planes to spread deadly germs. Just to be safe, the FAA banned crop dusting flights and ordered background checks on those pilots and crews.

State officials called out National Guard troops to help with the cleanup. By the end of the week, Congress, acting very quickly, approved $40 billion to fight terrorism and to aid in the recovery effort. A few days later Congress approved an appropriation of $20 billion to help the ailing airline companies.

Secretary of State Colin Powell began putting together an international coalition that would fight terrorism. Terrorist groups exist in more than sixty countries. Powell received a lot of support for the coalition, even from countries that had not been friends of the United States in the past, such as Pakistan and Iran. The members of the North Atlantic Treaty

Rescue workers sift through the wreckage of the World Trade Center.

Organization (NATO) declared that an attack on one member was an attack on all the members. The United Nations Security Council unanimously approved a US resolution demanding that all countries crack down on terrorism.

President Bush created a cabinet-level Department of Homeland Security. This office would coordinate the forty different agencies that are concerned with security on US soil. These agencies include the Border Patrol, Customs Service, Coast Guard, and Federal Emergency Management Agency.

The investigation into the attacks soon had a name: PENTTBOM—Pentagon Two Towers Bombing.

More Information Comes to Light

Some of the first information revealed heroic acts by the passengers on the plane that crashed in Pennsylvania. Several of the passengers had called family and friends on their cell phones to report they were being hijacked. When the callers learned that the World Trade Center towers and the Pentagon had been hit they knew that their plane was on its way to destroying something significant. Air traffic controllers heard scuffling and someone in the cockpit shouting, "Get out of here." Shortly after that, the passengers evidently overpowered the hijackers and caused the plane to crash in a wooded area.

The FBI quickly had an idea of which passengers had hijacked the planes. The nineteen suspects carried Middle Eastern passports. They left a trail of credit card receipts, rental car contracts, and hotel bills. Several of the hijackers had paid for flight training at schools in Florida. Agents checked out the training logs of these schools, looking for others who had enrolled at the same time.

THE HAMBURG CELL

Nineteen hijackers carried out the attacks on September 11, 2001. These men were divided into four different groups to take over the four planes. Each group had a trained pilot, who acted as the leader of the group. The other three or four hijackers aided the pilot by subduing the plane's crewmembers and passengers. Pilots were personally picked by Osama bin Laden because of their English language skills and familiarity with Western culture.

Members of the Hamburg cell included Mohammed Atta, Marwan al-Shehhi, and Ramzi bin al-Shibh.

Mohammed Atta was the pilot of American Airlines Flight 11 and, at thirty-three, the oldest of the hijackers. Born in the United Arab Emirates, he studied at the Hamburg Technical University in Germany. While there, Atta met fellow students Marwan al-Shehhi, who would become the pilot on United Airlines Flight 175, Ziad Jarrah, who would pilot United Airlines Flight 93, and Ramzi bin al-Shibh, who was supposed to participate in the September 11 attacks but could not gain entry to the United States. These men would meet several times a week to discuss their anti-American plans. In November 1999, the men traveled together to Afghanistamn and Pakistan to meet with Osama bin Laden. It was then that they received instructions for the attack and began to plan the September 11 attack. Because they had all met while studying at Hamburg Technical University, they became known as the Hamburg cell.

The hijacker who may have been the coordinator, Mohammed Atta, left behind a five-page document that appeared to be final instructions. It included Islamic prayers and urged the hijackers to crave death and be optimistic. They were to pray and recite the Koran on the night before the attacks. The document also included some practical advice: the men were to check their bags, IDs, knives, passports, and papers. They were instructed to make sure no one followed them. If they succeeded in carrying out their attacks, they would have eternal life.

CHAPTER FOUR

Al-Qaeda

Early on in the FBI's investigation, Osama bin Laden was their top suspect. A Saudi who had been hiding for five years in Afghanistan, bin Laden was suspected of having a part in many terrorist acts, including the 1993 bombing of the World Trade Center tower and the 1998 bombing of two US embassies in Africa. FBI investigators and terrorism experts believed that he was the only person who could have mastered the September 11 attacks. While bin Laden denied responsibility for the attacks for many years, a video surfaced in 2006 that allegedly shows him admitting to orchestrating them.

Bin Laden was born in Saudi Arabia in 1957. His father, a conservative Muslim, had four wives and fifty-two children. Bin Laden's father owned a construction company and became a favorite of the Saudi ruling family. He built a palace in Jiddah for the family and then won a contract to restore shrines in Mecca and Medina, the most holy places of Islam.

When bin Laden was in his early teens his father died. The young man inherited about $80 million and spent several years partying in Beirut and other places. After a time, bin Laden lost interest in this kind of life. He married and enrolled in King Aziz University in Jiddah, where he studied civil engineering. At the university he learned from scholars who believed that civil conflicts occurring in Lebanon were God's punishment for the depravity of Beirut.

Osama bin Laden was a Saudi millionaire and the founder of al-Qaeda.

Bin Laden did not feel close to his family and increasingly became interested in the Muslim Brotherhood. That group made him feel guilty about his youthful binges and turned him into a fundamentalist.

Bin Laden wanted to create a Muslim world on the Arab Peninsula that would be governed by divine justice and free of the decadent influence of the West. He thought that the United States supported his goal of making all of the area a Muslim state. After the war between the Soviet Union and Afghanistan ended, bin Laden realized that the only reason the United States had helped the mujahideen was to defeat its rival, the Soviet Union. When bin Laden realized he had been used, the United States became his new enemy.

THE BIN LADEN FAMILY

Osama bin Laden had six wives and fathered over twenty children. In 2009, his first wife, Najwa, and their son, Omar, coauthored a memoir titled *Growing Up Bin Laden: Osama's Wife and Son Take Us Inside Their Secret World.* Najwa, who had left bin Laden in 2001, described how the man she knew and married at the age of eighteen had transformed into one of the world's most wanted men. The book also describes their time in hiding in the late 1990s, as bin Laden gained worldwide attention for his terrorist activities, and includes family photos.

Al-Qaeda

In 1988, bin Laden set up a terrorist organization, al-Qaeda, or "the Base." The immediate aim of the group was to establish an Islamic government in Saudi Arabia and to expel US troops from the region. Al-Qaeda gave oppressed Muslims money and military training. Members of the al-Qaeda groups signed an agreement called a *bayat.* According to the bayat, members would go to a country where a jihad (holy war) had been declared and wait to be called on to help. While living in another country, these groups set up "sleeper" units. Members of these units became part of their new communities and didn't attract attention to themselves.

In 1990, during the Persian Gulf War, an angry bin Laden urged the Saudi government to get rid of US troops because they desecrated the lands of Islam. Bin Laden said his Afghan Arabs could train the Saudis

Al-Qaeda fighters participate in military training in 2001.

to protect themselves. He also suggested that his family's construction company could dig huge trenches along the border with Kuwait to stop invaders. The Prince of Saudi Arabia declined bin Laden's offer and instead welcomed the American troops.

After this rejection, bin Laden started criticizing the Saudi monarchy. In 1991, Saudi Arabia expelled bin Laden for attempting to smuggle weapons. Bin Laden fled to Sudan, where he continued to speak out against the United States. When the United States sent troops to Somalia in 1992 as part of a United Nations relief mission, bin Laden ordered his followers to attack American interests. In 1994, Saudi Arabia revoked his citizenship.

FBI agents investigating the 1993 bombing of the World Trade Center discovered that several of the men involved in that bombing had fought in the Afghanistan war. They also found records that Ramzi Yousef, the mastermind of the bombing, had phoned Osama bin Laden.

In 1996, under pressure from the United States and Saudi Arabia, Sudan expelled bin Laden. Bin Laden fled to Afghanistan where he found friends among the Taliban, the ruling group of the country. Osama bin Laden moved from cave to cave in the rugged mountains guarded by militants armed with machine guns.

The Taliban had taken control of the country when the Soviets left in 1989. Like Ramzi Yousef, members of the Taliban were conservative Sunni Muslims. They passed very strict laws, especially against women. Women had to wear burqas, tentlike coverings that reach from head to foot, except for a small mesh opening around the eyes. Under the Taliban, women could not hold jobs, go to school, be treated in hospitals, or go out of the house without a male relative. Men had to attend mosques and grow beards. There was no music or other leisure activities. To escape the repressive atmosphere, many Afghans fled to Pakistan, where close to two million refugees lived even before the terrorist attacks on the United States.

The Taliban refused to turn bin Laden over to the United States to be put on trial for the embassy bombings in Africa. After the September 11 attack on the World Trade Center, the United States again demanded that bin Laden be turned over. In response, the Taliban claimed that the Council of Afghan clerics had asked bin Laden to leave. However, the clerics did not tell him when he had to leave. Later, the Taliban claimed they did not know where bin Laden was hiding.

For many years, Osama bin Laden stayed in hiding. The US government continued its search for him and often received false tips about where bin Laden was located. Later, it was discovered that he traveled among Taliban

Residents of Abbottabad, Pakistan, congregate outside the house where Osama bin Laden was killed by American forces in 2011.

safe houses in both Afghanistan and Pakistan in the years following 2001. In 2005, bin Laden moved with his family to Abbottabad, Pakistan. Several years later, American intelligence officials tracked one of bin Laden's couriers to Abbottabad and, in 2010, they were able to confirm that he lived in a compound that was most likely built to hide "someone important." They believed that Osama bin Laden lived there. On May 2, 2011, after many years of preparation and planning, US Special Forces landed in Abbottabad and raided the compound, killing Osama bin Laden. After nearly ten years, the search for America's most wanted terrorist was over.

CHAPTER FIVE

Reactions Against Muslims

Immediately following September 11, many Americans searched for who was to blame for the horrific attacks. Since all of the hijackers were from the Middle East and followed an interpretation of Islam, Americans unfortunately began to strike out against anyone who looked Middle Eastern or who they believed was Muslim.

Many Muslim mosques across the country received threats that they would be burned. Local police provided them with extra protection. Middle Eastern and Muslim students reported being stared at. Some were sent threatening notes. Anti-Arab graffiti defaced buildings. Women who wore the hijab, the sacred Muslim scarf, were intimidated. In Tennessee, a Muslim woman was beaten on her way to worship. Businesses owned by Middle Easterners were vandalized and burned. In Arizona, a man was killed because he had dark skin and wore a turban. The man was not Muslim, but a Sikh from India.

Those of Middle Eastern descent who were born in the United States resented the accusations that they were any less American than others. Some quit wearing their headgear so they wouldn't be objects of hate. Legal immigrants didn't want to go to the Immigration and Naturalization Service to get papers or information they needed for fear that they would be questioned or arrested.

Americans demonstrate against anti-Muslim bigotry in 2015.

One reason for the hatred may be that many Americans don't understand Islam. One of the most difficult ideas for non-Muslims to understand is that of jihad. The Koran teaches that when Islam or Muslim lands are threatened, Muslims should protect themselves by conducting jihad of the sword. Islamic doctrine has many rules about jihads. Civilians are not to be killed, and terrorism is prohibited. A Muslim should fight only those who fight him. Women, children, and the elderly must be spared. The Koran also says that suicide is against God's word.

Just as different branches of Christianity and Judaism interpret the words of the Bible differently, different branches of Islam interpret the

ISLAMOPHOBIA

Islamophobia is prejudice against Muslims because of their religious affiliation. Many organizations have warned in recent years about an uptick in Islamophobic attacks, including personal threats and attacks, graffiti using hate speech, and setting fire to mosques. The organization Think Progress keeps a running list of recent Islamophobic attacks on their website. As of 2016, over one hundred such attacks have been listed in less than one year.

Koran differently. Even though the hijackers may have believed they were carrying out the teachings of the Koran, most Muslims reject the version of Islam that approves of terrorism.

Although many of the hijackers were Muslims, they were not typical Muslims. They followed a very extreme form of the religion. Some experts on Islam speculate that Muslim extremists resent the fact that US culture dominates the world. The extremists think the United States is a secular country. They fear that as the influence of the United States spreads, Muslims will lose their language, their religion, and their way of life.

Fundamentalist Muslims terrorists want to return to a time when society was free of what they consider to be moral decay. They don't like Israel because they think it is a decadent Western country that pushed the Palestinians out of their homeland. They resent seeing non-Muslims taking over Muslim territory. They are angry at the United States because

A mother and daughter attend a vigil for three Muslim students killed in Islamophobic attacks in 2015.

it supports Israel. Many groups may feel this way, but they do not resort to terrorism. The fundamentalist Muslims turned the concept of jihad into permission to wage their personal wars.

In the years since 2001, Muslims have continued to face prejudice and discrimination because of their religion. Many American Muslims have felt that they need to hide their religion because of fears or anger directed at them. Immediately following the attacks, New York Mayor Giuliani urged Americans to judge people by who they are rather than what they look like. In one of his press conferences on September 11, 2001, he said, "Hatred, prejudice, and bigotry are what caused this terrible tragedy, and the people of the city of New York should act differently." His words can and should be applied to all Americans, even though many years have now passed since September 11, 2001.

CHAPTER SIX

The Global Fight Against Terrorism

Following the attacks, the United States government knew that they were being drawn into a new kind of war, a war against terrorism. This would be especially challenging because terrorist cells operated in many countries around the world and were not rooted in one particular country. Unlike traditional warfare, this war would not be limited to one particular country, although the United States knew that they would need to root out both al-Qaeda and their allies the Taliban in Afghanistan. Furthermore, it would be nearly impossible to negotiate with terrorists as their anti-American beliefs were based in ideological, or religious, views in addition to political disagreements.

Another difficulty the government had in fighting this war was that the people involved in the September 11 attack represented a new kind of terrorist. In the past, suicide terrorists were men in their late teens and early twenties who had been born into poverty, were fundamentalist in their religion, and didn't know much about the outside world. These terrorist groups bragged to the world about their attacks, even taking credit for attacks in which they had no part. Twenty-seven groups claimed credit for the 1993 World Trade Center bombing, for example.

The hijackers of the US planes, however, were generally older, educated, and technically skilled. They knew enough about the United States to live among its citizens without arousing any suspicions. No country or group took credit for the attack.

US soldiers take cover as a helicopter lands nearby while fighting in Khost Province, Afghanistan, in 2009.

The War in Afghanistan

The first thing the Bush administration did to fight the terrorists was cut off access to their money. The president signed an order freezing the assets of Osama bin Laden and other people and organizations connected to him. His actions stopped some of the money, but not all of it.

The military response to the attacks was called Operation Enduring Freedom. The Pentagon sent warplanes and aircraft carrier battle groups to the Persian Gulf. Several thousand reservists were called up to active duty. One problem for the military was that no one really knew who or what it was fighting. When the Japanese attacked Pearl Harbor in World War II, the United States knew who to attack—a country with armed forces. In the fight against terrorism, military leaders had no specific country or group to go after. However, they knew that they would have to focus on Afghanistan, where most of al-Qaeda's leadership and training camps were located.

In late 2001, American military forces invaded Afghanistan after Taliban leaders refused to extradite Osama bin Laden to the United States and to shut down terrorist bases. The country had been in the midst of a violent civil war since 1996, which had allowed Taliban forces to take control and provided safe haven for al-Qaeda. The United States government publically stated that its aim was to remove the Taliban from power in order to begin to dismantle the al-Qaeda leadership. In 2003, North Atlantic Trade Organization (NATO) members agreed to join the United States in their fight against terrorism in Afghanistan and brought in troops from forty-two different countries. British forces had already been helping American forces in Afghanistan as one of the United States closest allies since the beginning of the war.

The war in Afghanistan would go on to become the longest war ever in American history, lasting from 2001 until 2014. The Taliban was officially removed from power in December 2001, although it has since regrouped into a powerful insurgency group that continues to fight against the American-supported Afghani government. While American and British troops were officially withdrawn in 2014, fighting against the Taliban and al-Qaeda continues in the country. As of 2015, ten thousand American troops are in Afghanistan to conduct airstrikes and special operations raids. The fight against terrorist operatives in Afghanistan has proved to be a long and discouraging one with no clear end in sight.

THE ISLAMIC STATE

The Islamic State in Iraq and Syria (ISIS) began in 1999 as a subsidiary group of al-Qaeda in Iraq. In 2003, the group began fighting American forces in the country. In 2011, the Islamic State joined fighting in Syria

When Saddam Hussein was removed from power in Iraq, it caused a power vacuum in the country that enabled the rise of ISIS.

during the country's civil war and gained significantly more members. When the Islamic State entered back into Iraq in 2014, they had a loyal following, a financial base, and many weapons. They successfully captured several important Iraqi cities, including Mosul, and quickly gained global attention for their barbaric practices and their practice of targeting civilians.

The War in Iraq

The war in Afghanistan was not the only war that began largely in response to the September 11 attacks. For many years, tension existed between the United States and Iraq following the Persian Gulf War in 1990. Following the September 11 attacks, President Bush stated that he believed that the president of Iraq, Saddam Hussein, "harbored and supported terrorists" and had developed weapons of mass destruction. The attacks were largely used as a reason why the American military should invade Iraq.

In March 2003, American forces, along with British, Australian, and Polish coalition forces, entered Iraq. This was the beginning of the 2003 Iraq War, which lasted until December 2011. However, there is no evidence—and, indeed, no reason to believe—that Iraq ever supported terrorists or developed weapons of mass destruction. The war led to the deaths of many people and greatly destabilized the country. Although the United States officially ended the war in 2014, the country has since descended into chaos and given rise to many more terrorist groups,

In 2016, operations continued to remove ISIS from their last major stronghold in Iraq.

including the Islamic State in Iraq and Syria (ISIS). ISIS developed during the war from the terrorist organization al-Qaeda in Iraq and has since become the largest threat facing America and other countries today. In fact, ISIS has become more powerful than al-Qaeda and has taken over large areas of land both in Iraq and in the neighboring country of Syria. American forces have reentered Iraq to aid in its current civil conflict and the US government acknowledges that one of their most formidable battles is fighting against ISIS. ISIS and ISIS operatives have carried out many significant terrorist attacks across the world in recent years, including in cities such as Brussels, Paris, and Istanbul.

Terrorism Today

Many years after the September 11 attacks, the war on terrorism continues. It may be disheartening and even frightening to think that this is not a problem that will be easily solved. However, it is an important fight and the United States and its allies have won important victories along the way. As this book is heading to press, Iraqi forces with American aid are pushing ISIS out of their last major stronghold in Iraq. Other military battles surely remain on the horizon in the war against terrorism. However, another battle is being waged at home in the way Americans view and treat Muslims in the face of Islamic fundamentalism. Now, Americans must continue in their resolve that the legacy of September 11, 2001, will not be a legacy of hate.

Timeline

1989 Osama bin Laden founds al-Qaeda to fight against the Soviets in Afghanistan.

1993 On February 26, a bomb explodes in the underground garage of the World Trade Center, killing six and injuring over one thousand. An associate of bin Laden, Ramzi Yousef, is convicted of the attack.

1996 Osama bin Laden is expelled from Sudan and moves the al-Qaeda headquarters to Afghanistan.

1996 The Taliban takes control of Afghanistan.

1998 Bombs laid by al-Qaeda explode at US embassies in Kenya and Tanzania, killing 231 people.

2000 Two al-Qaeda suicide bombers attack the USS *Cole*, killing seventeen American sailors.

2001 Four planes are hijacked by al-Qaeda operatives and crashed into the World Trade Center, the Pentagon, and a field in Shanksville, Pennsylvania, killing nearly three thousand people. In October, American forces invade Afghanistan.

2003 Khalid Shaikh Mohammed, a suspected plotter of the September 11 attacks, is arrested by Pakistani and US agents; American forces invade Iraq.

2004 Bombs planted by al-Qaeda members on commuter trains in Madrid, Spain, kill 190 people; In a video, Osama bin Laden claims direct responsibility for the 2001 attacks.

2006 Zacarias Moussaoui is found guilty of terrorism charges in his role in the September 11 attacks and is sentenced to life in prison; al-Qaeda in Iraq is renamed the Islamic State in Iraq.

2011 Osama bin Laden is killed during a US Special Forces raid on his compound in Abottabad, Pakistan.

2013 The Islamic State in Iraq renames itself the Islamic State in Iraq and Syria (ISIS) after joining fighting in Syria's civil war.

2014 ISIS gains territory in Iraq; al-Qaeda distances itself from ISIS, disagreeing with its extreme tactics; American forces begin airstrikes against ISIS.

2016 Iraqi forces launch operation to regain the last ISIS stronghold, Mosul.

Glossary

airstrikes An attack by air, such as bombs dropped by a fighter jet.

appropriation Funds set aside by a group such as the government for a specific purpose.

bigotry Intolerance against those who are different than oneself.

bunker An underground room that is often built of reinforced concrete. It is designed for protection during military attacks.

coalition A temporary alliance among countries in order to act together on a problem that affects everyone in the group.

desecrate To violate the sacredness of a holy place or object.

evacuate To remove someone from a dangerous area to a safe place.

forensics The use of medicine to solve legal questions. Often, this means the analysis of a cause of death.

formidable Arousing fear, dread, or awe.

freeze assets To put a block on a bank account so the account holder cannot withdraw money.

fundamentalist Someone who follows the literal meaning of a religious text.

grandeur Splendor of appearance.

ground zero The place directly where an explosion has occurred.

guerillas Small independent military groups that fight informally.

hijab The headscarf some Muslim women wear.

hijack To take over an aircraft or other vehicle by force in order to direct it to a different destination.

intelligence Information gathered that concerns an enemy.

Islamic State in Iraq and Syria (ISIS) A terrorist organization that emerged from Iraq and Syria following the 2003 Iraq War.

Islamophobia Prejudice against Muslims because of their religion.

jihad Holy war.

monotheistic Believing that only one god exists.

mujahideen Muslim freedom fighters.

operative A person who does secret work for a government or organization.

secular Things that relate to the world rather than to religion.

secure communications A place where phone messages, faxes, and other electronic communications can't be intercepted.

shrine A place that is considered sacred by a religious group. It is often a place where a ritual is performed.

subsidiary A branch of a larger company or organization

Taliban An Islamic fundamentalist group that controlled Afghanistan until American forces pushed them out in 2001.

weapons of mass destruction Chemical, biological, or nuclear weapons capable of causing widespread devastation.

For More Information

American Civil Liberties Union (ACLU)
125 Broad Street, 18th Floor
New York, NY 10004
(212) 549-2500
Website: http://www.aclu.org
The ACLU is a nonprofit organization that seeks to preserve individual rights and liberties for all American citizens as guaranteed by the Constitution. The ACLU employs lawyers, lobbyists, and community organizers.

Anti-Defamation League (ADL)
605 3rd Avenue
New York, NY 10158
(212) 885-7700
Website: http://www.adl.org
The ADL was founded in 1913 to "stop the defamation of the Jewish people and to secure justice and fair treatment to all." Now, the ADL fights all forms of bigotry in order to provide equal rights for all.

Electronic Frontier Foundation (EEF)
454 Shotwell Street
San Francisco, CA 94110
(415) 436-9333
Website: http://www.eff.org
The EEF is the top nonprofit organization for defending people's rights online. The organization works to provide safe and secure internet

access to all, defends free speech online, and fights for anti-surveillance laws.

Electronic Privacy Information Center (EPIC)
1718 Connecticut Avenue, NW, Suite 200
Washington, DC 20009
(202) 483-1140
Website: http://www.epic.org
EPIC is a public interest research center that focuses on protecting civil rights and privacy issues in the information age. EPIC staff work in policy research, public education, litigation, and advocacy.

Federal Bureau of Investigation (FBI)
935 Pennsylvania Avenue NW
Washington, DC 20535
(202) 324-3000
Website: http://www.fbi.gov
The FBI is the United States's national security organization that is tasked with both intelligence and law enforcement responsibilities. FBI agents and analysts work to protect the United States from terrorism and other major criminal threats.

US Department of Homeland Security (DHS)
12th and C Street SW
Washington, DC 20024
(202) 282-8000
Website: https://www.dhs.gov
The DHS was created in the wake of the September 11 terrorist attacks in order to provide a coordinated response to potential terrorist threats in

the United States. Today, the DHS has 240,000 employees who work in jobs ranging from border security, to terrorism, to emergency response.

US Department of Justice (DOJ)
950 Pennsylvania Avenue, NW
Washington, DC 20530
(202) 514-2000
Website: https://www.justice.gov
The DOJ is part of the executive branch of the federal government and is responsible for enforcing the law and administering justice in the United States. The attorney general heads this department.

Websites

Because of the changing nature of internet links, Rosen Publishing has developed an online list of websites related to the subject of this book. This site is updated regularly. Please use this link to access the list:

http://www.rosenlinks.com/TER21/worldtrade

For Further Reading

Aslan, Reza. *No god but God: The Origins and Evolution of Islam.* New York, NY: Ember, 2012.

Friedman, Lauri S. *Terrorism* (Introducing Issues With Opposing Viewpoints). New York, NY: Greenhaven Press, 2010.

Green, Robert. *Cause & Effect: The September 11 Attacks* (Cause & Effect in History). San Diego, CA: ReferencePoint Press, 2015.

Hillstrom, Kevin. *The September 11 Terrorist Attacks* (Defining Moments). Detroit, MI: Omnigraphics, Inc., 2012.

Mills, Wendy. *All We Have Left.* New York, NY: Bloomsbury, 2016.

Morell, Michael, and Bill Harlow. *The Great War of Our Time: The CIA's Fight Against Terrorism—From al Qa'ida to ISIS.* New York, NY: Twelve, 2016.

Parker Rhodes, Jewell. *Towers Falling.* New York, NY: Little, Brown Books for Young Readers, 2016.

Polisner, Gae. *The Memory of Things.* New York, NY: St. Martin's Griffin, 2016.

Schmermund, Elizabeth. *Domestic Terrorism* (At Issue). New York, NY: Greenhaven Press, 2017.

Silverstein, Adam J. *Islamic History: A Very Short Introduction.* New York, NY: Oxford UP, 2010.

Wong, Adam. *The World Trade Center* (History's Great Structures). San Diego, CA: ReferencePoint Press, 2013.

Bibliography

Beyer, Lisa. "The Most Wanted Man in the World." *Time*, September 24, 2001. http://content.time.com/time/magazine/article/0,9171,1000871,00.html.

Constable, Pamela. "Taliban: Bin Laden Told to Leave." *Washington Post*, September 28, 2001.

Darton, Eric. *Divided We Stand: A Biography of the World Trade Center*. New York, NY: Basic Books, Perseus Books Group, 1999.

"Death, Destruction, Charity, Salvation, War, Money, Real Estate, Spouses, Babies, and Other September 11 Statistics." *New York*, September 2014. http://nymag.com/news/articles/wtc/1year/numbers.htm.

Dwyer, Jim, David Kocieniewski, Deidre Murphy, and Peg Tyre. *Two Seconds Under the World*. New York, NY: Crown Publishers, 1994.

Elliott, Michael. "Retaliation War." *Time*, September 24, 2001.

Hanna, Mike. "The Connection Between Iraq and 9/11." *Al Jazeera*, September 7, 2011. http://www.aljazeera.com/indepth/spotlight/the911decade/2011/09/2011971555513938336.html.

John, Tara. "Timeline: The Rise of ISIS." *Time*, October 9, 2015. http://time.com/4030714/isis-timeline-islamic-state.

Kaplan, David E., and Kevin Whitelaw. "The CEO of Terror, Inc." *U. S. News & World Report*, October 1, 2001.

McGeary, Johanna, and David van Biema. "The New Breed of Terrorism." *Time*, September 24, 2001.

Moss, Michael, and Charles Bagli. "Workers Say They Were Instructed Not to Leave Doomed South Tower." *New York Times*, September 13, 2001.

Murphy, Caryle. "Terrorists' Islam Not Condoned." *Washington Post*, September 17, 2001.

Ochs, Ridgley. "Decade Later, Trauma Haunts 9/11 Survivors." *Newsday*, September 7, 2011. http://www.newsday.com/911-anniversary/decade-later-trauma-haunts-9-11-survivors-1.3152854.

Reeve, Simon. *The New Jackals*. Boston, MA: Northeastern University Press, 1999.

Rempel, William C., and Richard A. Serrano. "U.S. on Terrorists' Trail." *Los Angeles Times*, September 13, 2001.

Rosin, Hanna. "Arab-Americans Familiar with Being Usual Suspects." *Washington Post*, September 14, 2001.

Stein, Joel. "Digging Out." *Time*, September 24, 2001. http://content.time.com/time/magazine/article/0,9171,1000879,00.html.

"U.S. War in Afghanistan: Timeline." *Council on Foreign Relations*. Retrieved November 3, 2016. http://www.cfr.org/afghanistan/us-war-afghanistan/p20018.

Woodward, Bob. "Hijacker Left Behind Eerie Instructions." *Washington Post*, September 28, 2001.

Woodward, Bob, and Walter Pincus. "FBI Knew of Al-Qaeda Groups in U.S." *Washington Post*, September 17, 2001.

Index

About the Authors

Lena Koya is a writer and scholar who lives in New York with her family. She researches literature about the 2003 Iraq War and enjoys writing about current events for teenagers.

Carolyn Gard is a former teacher and writer who writes mainly for teenagers. In addition, she does research for members of the Colorado state legislature. She lives in Boulder, Colorado, where she enjoys hiking with her German shepherds.

Photo Credits

Cover, p. 1 New York Daily News/Getty Images; back cover and interior pages background aleksandr hunta/Shutterstock.com (smoke), Alex Gontar/Shutterstock.com (grunge); p. 5 Larry Bruce/Shutterstock.com; pp. 8-9 Joseph Sohm/Shutterstock.com; p. 12 José Nicholas/Corbis Historical/Getty Images; p. 14 Porter Gifford/Hulton Archive/Getty Images; p. 16 Jeffrey Markowitz/Sygma/Getty Images; pp. 19, 35 CNN/3rd Party - Misc/Getty Images; p. 20-–21 Aaron Milestone/AFP/Getty Images; p. 23 Catrina Genovese/The LIFE Images Collection/Getty Images; pp. 26, 30 Mario Tama/Getty Images; p. 27 Paul J. Richards/AFP/Getty Images; p. 32 DDP/AFP/Getty Images; p. 37 Al Rai Al Aam/Feature Story News/Getty Images; p. 39 The Asahi Shimbun/Getty Images; p. 41 Mandel Ngan/AFP/Getty Images; p. 43 Mark Ralston/AFP/Getty Images; p. 46 Jonathan Saruk/Getty Images; p. 48 Pierre Perrin/Gamma-Rapho/Getty Images; p. 50 Anadolu Agency/Getty Images.

Designer: Nicole Russo-Duca; Editor: Elizabeth Schmermund;
Photo Researcher: Elizabeth Schmermund